RUGBY AND CRICKET
FOR
MUMS

RUGBY AND CRICKET
FOR
MUMS

A brief introduction to rugby and cricket
for mums and all other supporters
new to the games

A. SUE PORTER
Illustrations by Amanda Stiby

SOUVENIR PRESS

First published 1995 by
Souvenir Press Ltd,
43 Great Russell Street, London WC1B 3PA
and simultaneously in Canada

ISBN 0 285 63302 3

Photoset by Rowland Phototypesetting Ltd,
Bury St Edmunds, Suffolk

Printed in Great Britain by
Biddles Ltd, Guildford and King's Lynn

Part One of this book, with variations in the text and
different illustrations, was first published privately in 1994
by Caterham School, Surrey, under the title *Rugby for Mums*.

This book is dedicated to that hardy band of supporters (but mostly mothers) who brave all the weather that the British Isles can throw at them, either to watch a bunch of grubby small boys doing their best to kill each other (or so it seems to the uninitiated), or, in spring and summer, to watch not a lot happening—unless their sons (or daughters) are among the few experts who can actually play the game of cricket with the style and grace that nature intended.

Contents

Acknowledgements 9
Introduction 11

PART ONE: RUGBY FOR MUMS
What is Rugby? 15
Your Son's Position 18
  Rugby Playing Positions 19
  So Now He Has a Position—What Happens Next? 25
The Game 27
  The Pitch 27
  Playing a Game 29
  Infringements Various 36
Mum's Notes 40
  Game Scores 41

PART TWO: CRICKET FOR MUMS
What is Cricket? 45
  A Cricket History Lesson 46
Terminology for Beginners 49
An Introduction to the Game 55
  Preparing a Field for Cricket 55
  The Aims of the Game 57
Equipment Needed to Play Cricket 61
Playing a Game 65
  Limited-Over Cricket 66

Getting Out, or Losing a Wicket   69
The Players and Their Skills   76
   Bowlers   76
   Fielding Positions   80
   Batting Techniques   84
Mum's Work   88
   Mum's Essential Equipment   90
Some Other Cricketing Terms   93
Scoring   96
   Umpire's Signals   102
Afterthought   104

Acknowledgements

The author would like to thank:

Caterham School, whose myriad sporting activities inspired the writing of this book as a guide to its bewildered mums.

Stephen Smith, Headmaster of Caterham School for over 21 years, and a former England scrum-half, without whose support this book would probably never have been published, for his advice on the game of rugby.

John Moulton, House Master at Caterham School and cricket umpire, whose invaluable advice ensured the accuracy of the information in the cricket section, along with Alistair Tapp, master in charge of cricket at Caterham School.

Zoe Chambers and Daphne Sales, without whom the author's knowledge of a cricketing mum's life would not have been complete.

And last but never least, Dad and David, without whom my interest in both these games would never have been kindled in the first place, and Gareth and Alan for giving me a reason to stand on touch lines and sit by boundaries for the past seven years!

Introduction

Why write a book on rugby and cricket for mums? I must have been asked this question more times than bear thinking about since the appearance of my first booklet on the game of rugby. That was designed to inform and entertain the parents of Caterham School in Surrey, where my own two boys enjoy multiple sporting activities in the guise of education.

There are of course many detailed books on the rules and techniques for playing both cricket and rugby, but few of them are aimed specifically at the spectator—and none at mums in particular.

Any mum who has stood in the freezing cold on a rugby touch line will confirm that the more you learn about the game, the more enjoyable watching a match becomes. So it was for me, and as my elder son's team was supported by parents with boys farther up the school, whose knowledge was greater than mine, I was only too grateful for small crumbs of wisdom that they passed on to me during the course of school matches. As the years progressed I gradually felt I was beginning to understand this exciting sport and in my turn I passed on some of my knowledge to the spectators watching my smaller son's matches. It was these good souls who kept saying, 'Why don't you write a book about it?'

As my knowledge of cricket increased, and especially when I learned how to score and could concentrate fully on the match in progress, I developed a great love of this summer game, too.

Despite attending my father's cricket matches for over 15 years during my childhood, I had never really concentrated on what was taking place on the field, except to applaud the taking of wickets or excellent batting when fours and sixes were scored. It was therefore the encouragement of other cricketing mothers (some of whom had sons who have gone on to play for county and country) that inspired me to want to find out more.

So it was these experiences that inspired me to write this book which I hope all new supporters, not just mums, will find helpful. If your son, grandson, nephew or godson has recently taken up one of these sports which you were not able to play yourself, for whatever reason, hopefully the explanations in this book will improve your enjoyment and understanding of what are two fine team games, enjoyed not just by the players but by loyal bands of spectators too. And if your new boyfriend is insisting on your accompanying him to watch his favourite pastime, the information in this book will help you to understand what he and his friends are actually doing.

PART ONE

RUGBY FOR MUMS

'My Baby's Playing Rugby'

What is Rugby?

The game of Rugby Football, so history tells us, started in 1823 when William Webb Ellis (a pupil at Rugby School) picked up a football and ran with it. This was the start of amateur Rugby Union football, which also led to the development of the professional game of Rugby League.

Since those early days the game has progressively been refined and improved and is now governed by rules and regulations known as 'Laws', some of which I shall attempt to explain to the layman/woman in these pages. Since your sons will be playing what has until recently been the game of amateur rugby or Rugby Union, I shall be explaining all the laws relating to that game; however, many of the laws of Union also apply to League football and you may watch a Rugby League match on television with new eyes after reading this book.

The main aim of the game is to score points. This is done by the team carrying, passing and kicking the ball to the opposition's try line and touching the ball down behind the line to score a *try*. This is then *converted* if a player can kick the ball over the crossbar, between the posts, having previously placed it back on the pitch in line with the point where the try was scored. If the kick is successful more points are added. Alternatively, the ball can be kicked over the posts from a penalty kick or as a drop kick (kicking the ball after dropping it from your hands) in order to score points.

There is little use in telling you what the numbers of points are for each of these methods of scoring, since the Rugby Football Union seems to change them at regular intervals, so I suggest you ask your son to let you know at the beginning of each season what the current points scores are. I have included a useful notes section at the end of Part One for you to mark down the current points system and keep a tally of your son's team's progress.

Any changes at the senior end of the game, resulting from the move to professionalism, will not, one hopes, affect the junior players, and so the descriptions of amateur rugby given in this book should apply to your son's game for some time to come.

Scoring a try

The team is divided into two main categories of player:

1 The **forwards** are responsible for getting the ball down the pitch using brute strength and techniques known as

rucking, mauling and scrummaging, all of which will be explained in more detail later. One of the most common forms of organised play you will see is a type of group hug, a male bonding practice properly called a scrummage (or scrum).

2 The **backs** run with the ball, passing it between themselves and running down the pitch until they are tackled by the opposition, whereupon they must immediately pass, or release the ball to the ground. The ball must always be passed backwards (away from the direction in which the players are running). If the ball is passed forwards to a member of the team this is called a *forward pass* and is penalised by the opposition getting to put the ball in at a scrum.

The forwards can also run with the ball and the backs can join in the rucking and mauling, but both tend to avoid playing each other's type of game.

In the following pages I shall try to explain as simply as possible the many other rules and techniques involved in playing rugby football.

Your Son's Position

Almost the first question every mum will ask her son after he starts playing rugby is: 'What position are you playing?'

This demonstration of knowledge usually leads to you falling flat on your face when your son replies, 'I don't know—I think I'm a *back* (or I think I'm a *forward*).' Since the game is new to him as well, it may take some weeks before he actually plays regularly in the same position on the field, and during this time he will have no idea whatsoever what position he plays! Eventually, however, he will become part of the regular *back* line or become a *forward*.

At this early age it is usually the larger children who become forwards and the smaller or faster ones who become backs. Later this position may be reversed as they grow and change shape with teenage, and your slim little back may turn into a hulking brute of a forward over the space of a couple of rugby seasons.

However, it will generally remain true that if he is fast across the ground he will become a back and if he towers above his peers or weighs a little more than average he will be more suited to the forward lines.

The smallest player on the pitch is usually the scrum half. Quite why the smallest player should be the one who has to get closest to the big, heavy forwards I have never understood, but there it is.

RUGBY PLAYING POSITIONS

Unlike an Association Football team of 11 players, rugby teams consist of 15. These are split almost equally between *backs* and *forwards*. Certain positions on the rugby pitch require particular physiques, and the following descriptions may help you to pick out a player at a glance as you start to watch your first season of rugby.

The front row
Tight-head prop   Hooker   Loose-head prop

The Forwards

They consist of:

The Front Row Forwards

These include the *Hooker* and the *Prop Forwards* (*Tight-head* and *Loose-head*). Tradition has it that forwards do not need the looks of a Hollywood film star to play well. To be an effective front row forward a player should preferably have very long arms and no neck. Players with normal arms and necks tend to play elsewhere—regardless of their looks!

Front row forwards are renowned for their volatile natures—they are best left well alone as they can become awkward if roused!

Prop forward   Second row forward

The Second Row Forwards (Locks)

The second row forwards help keep the scrum together, but their main claim to fame on the field is the ability to use their extra height in line-outs. It is this extra height that also gives them their other reputation—that of being highly sociable. Their ability to catch a barmaid's eye is developed much earlier than their peers', as is their ability to hoodwink a barman into believing they are over the drinking age limit. They can thus be relied on to get in a round of drinks no matter who is paying— merely asking a pint as fee for this service. No wonder they join in the end-of-match celebrations earlier than the rest of the team.

The Back Row Forwards

These are made up of *Number 8* and two *Flankers* or *Wing Forwards*. The back row are supposed to be able to use their brains as well as their brawn. Flankers are the enemy of the opposition half-backs whose lives are under constant threat from their crunching tackles. The number 8 keeps the scrum together and controls the release of the ball once it has been heeled back through the scrum by the hooker—at least that is the theory! At this stage it is more likely that they just didn't like having someone's head stuffed up their backside and choose to stand at the back out of personal preference.

Incidentally, flankers have a well-deserved reputation for being excellent blood donors. Sadly, little of this makes it as far as the transfusion service, most being spilt over rugby shirts and fields, so if play is stopped for an injury it's a pretty good bet that the player on the floor will be a bleeding flanker—assuming the full back is not involved!

The Backs

They consist of:

The Wingers and the Inside and Outside Centres
These are the *Three-quarters*, made up of the inside and outside centres and the wingers—four players in all. Whilst the centres get to move around either side of the fly half (see below) the two wingers generally remain on their respective sides of the pitch throughout the game until they get the ball. The wingers certainly think of themselves as the Linford Christies of the rugby squad and spend hours running up and down the pitch, hardly ever touching the ball. The inside and outside centres try to use their intelligence to decide which way to pass the ball to avoid being tackled by the opposition, and one frequently looks upon himself as a crash ball specialist and will set up attacks and give his team mates passes which will result in *their* permanent disability rather than his own.

The Half-backs
These are the *Fly Half* (or *Outside Half*) and the *Scrum Half*. Both the scrum half and the fly half think they are in charge.

A winger

They care about things like ball pressure (a soft ball bounces less well than a well pumped-up version). They discuss crosswinds and options, things the majority couldn't give a toss about. Generally they are regarded as more intelligent than the others and are expected to make end-of-season reports on behalf of their team.

As I previously pointed out, the scrum half is usually the smallest person on the pitch. He will be the one you see throwing the ball at the feet of the group hug (scrum) and then dashing to the back of this group to pick the ball out again (now doesn't that seem such a waste of time!?) in order to throw it back to the fly half who may pass it on to the three-quarters.

This is frequently done with what looks like an attempt on his part to defy gravity and fly, which leads to him landing flat on the ground in the mud whilst the forwards rampage over the top of him to get to the ball. As a result he is often the person with the most understanding mother, as his kit will usually be the dirtiest (except perhaps for the full back—see below).

The scrum half

Last but not least, the Full Back

He seemingly enjoys getting stamped all over by the opposition as he cleanly catches high balls. He bounces up from the heap of players, waving away any trainer who might want to treat any wounds he has sustained in the process, and having cleared the ball by kicking it back down the pitch, he will search the skies again for the next high ball to catch. He really hopes this will give him a chance to run back at the opposition, despite the high risk of being trampled under foot yet again as the attacking team chases after the ball.

If your son frequently returns from rugby claiming that the rest of the team have blamed him for losing the match, it is a pretty certain bet that he is a full back.

As the last line of defence for the team, if all the others have failed to stop a marauding attack from the opposition, he can be relied on to throw himself selflessly at the feet of the thundering attacker in a desperate attempt to halt his progress towards the try line. All too frequently, however, he will fail as

The 'brave' full back

his opposite number is likely to be a) heavier, b) taller and c)
coming at speed.

SO NOW HE HAS A POSITION—WHAT HAPPENS NEXT?

Initially younger children will learn to pass the ball and will play *touch rugby*. Just to save us mums from worrying too much, this means that they will not be learning how to tackle (or bring down) their opponents just yet but will just touch them lightly with a hand in order to force them to pass the ball to another player on their own team, or failing that they will have to give the ball to the opposition.

However, touch rugby does not last for ever and before long he will be tackling his friends and crashing to the ground with them—this is known as the start of *the washing season*.

Once he has mastered tackling, your washing load will instantly increase as his muddy rugby shorts, socks and shirt are brought home after every games lesson (and practice) and are needed, clean and pressed, frequently for the next day! The advantages of having a second string (or perhaps second-hand) set of clothes to save the panic washing and drying of kit will rapidly become apparent. Of course some boys seem able to play in mud-caked, hardened kit from day to day without ever bringing it home, but the masters soon put a stop to this and suggest adding to mum's washing is preferable to gassing the rest of the team.

If you are lucky (and the games masters continue to hold sway) your son will have a shower after each rugby session and at least *he* will return home clean. If you are not so lucky, he will change quickly into his school uniform before anyone notices he has not showered and you will note him scratching his legs whilst trying to do his prep. At this stage I suggest you insist that he shows you his mud-covered limbs and then force him upstairs to the bathroom. The earlier you can catch him, the less fine mud dust will be found on the carpet the next morning!

The start of the washing season

The Game

Well, now you have a feel for what is going on, it is time to have a go at describing the game itself, and just to make things easy let's start by describing the ground on which it is played—the *Pitch*.

THE PITCH

A rugby pitch is divided into several sections. At each end there is a section behind the goal posts marked by a white line. Between the edge of the pitch, on the goal line level with the posts and through to this line is where a try can be scored. The goal line may also be called the *try line*, while the line behind the posts is called the *dead ball line*. In other words, if the ball keeps on going until it passes the dead ball line it is no longer in play and no one can score by touching it down here.

In addition to the try area the pitch is marked with a centre line and spot through which the kick-off is taken. There are also twenty-two metre lines and ten metre lines as shown on the diagram and along the length of the pitch there are lines marked at five and fifteen metres into the pitch.

Turn to the next page for a rough idea of what a rugby pitch looks like from a spectactor's point of view.

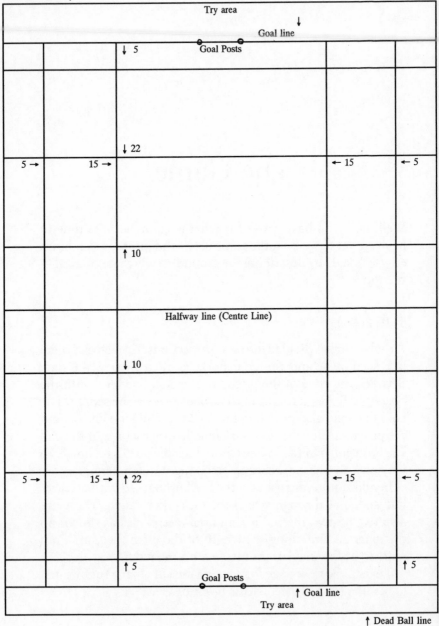

Dead Ball line ↓

Try area

Goal line ↓

↓ 5   Goal Posts

↓ 22

5 →   15 →   ← 15   ← 5

↑ 10

Halfway line (Centre Line)

↓ 10

5 →   15 →   ↑ 22   ← 15   ← 5

↑ 5   ↑ 5

Goal Posts

↑ Goal line

Try area

↑ Dead Ball line

Touch line

A Rugby pitch

PLAYING A GAME

Once our player has mastered the basic rules of passing and tackling, the more complicated rules and regulations will start to enter into his skills.

Touching Down—Scoring a Touch Down or Try

To touch the ball down the player carrying the ball merely has to push it down on the grass inside the try area. He can also do this by diving towards the ground with it in his hands. Alternatively, if the ball has been kicked over the line, he can race after it and dive towards it and slap it down with his hand or hands. The vision of a speeding half-back racing over the line and launching himself at the ball is one of the funnier sights available to watching mums and dads, perhaps only bettered by the sight of a scrum half trying to peer over the shoulders or through the legs of a particularly large second-row forward to see where a ball has gone in a scrum or line-out.

Forward Play

For forwards this will include *line-outs*, *mauls* and *rucks* as well as *scrums*. The main role of the forwards is to wrest the ball from the opposition through these various techniques.

If a ball goes off the side of the pitch (known as the side line) a *line-out* will be taken.

Line-outs

Many disagreements will occur at the start of a *line-out* since it is not the team that kicked or threw the ball out who will throw it back in, it is their opposition (as in football).

However, once it has been established which team is taking the *throw-in*, it is the hooker's job to throw the ball, straight, over the heads of the two rows of forwards. The forwards from each team must stand next to each other in two straight lines about one metre or three feet apart. Meanwhile the opposition hooker has to stand next to the throwing hooker until the ball has been thrown.

A regular line-out will have seven forwards in each line.

A short line-out can reduce this number to as few as two in each line.

Once the ball has been thrown by the hooker, the forwards all jump to try to catch it as it passes over their heads. Ideally, one of them will catch the ball and will then turn his back on the opposition and set up a maul or a ruck (see p. 33) until the ball emerges to be passed to the scrum half. Alternatively, they can *tap* the ball down to the scrum half. However, if they do this they are only allowed to use either their inside arm or both arms. Once the scrum half has the ball he will, hopefully, pass it out to the fly half and on to the backs for them to *run the ball*.

The line-out is a place where many infringements can occur (pushing, lifting, and worse as your son's career develops). If, after a line-out, the ball is immediately handed to the other team to kick, you can guarantee that your son's team committed one of these infringements.

If the hooker is asked to throw again, it may be that he did not manage to throw the ball in straight over the lines of forwards (when your son is still learning the game, referees will frequently let them have *a second go*). Once the rules have been learned, however, the opposition are offered the choice of a scrum or another line-out and this time *their* hooker will get to throw or put the ball in.

The sort of minor infringement which would result in a scrum being taken could be a *knock-on* (where one of the team drops the ball forwards onto the ground). *Knock-ons* also occur when backs are running with the ball and passing it to another back who does not quite catch the ball but drops it forwards.

Scrums (or group hugs)
A scrum occurs after a foul has taken place (forward passes, knock-ons, un-straight throw-ins, accidental offside, etc.). All

the backs, except the scrum half, retreat away from the position of the scrum and leave the forwards to get on with it.

The forwards line up as shown below. Some sets of rugby shirts are numbered to tally with the positions in the scrum.

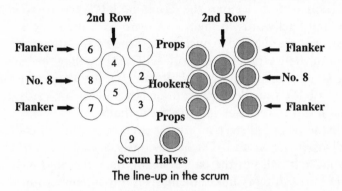

The line-up in the scrum

If your son wants to tape his ears down before playing rugby, don't be surprised. The pain that he could incur as his fellow forwards hug him, crushing their hips into his head, or as he crashes his head against the opposition heads as the scrum comes together, will rapidly convince you that taping his ears is the least of his problems. However, it should be noted that most forwards are not masochistic enough to do this and only the *hardest* amongst the boys will take to taping their ears from an early age.

Taping the ears to play

The scrum half who is to place the ball into the scrum stands to the left side of his own hooker with his opposition scrum half next to him (see diagram). Once the scrum has formed the forwards all brace themselves and wait for the ball to be *put in*. As soon as the ball enters the scrum, both hookers try to *hook* the ball backwards to their own team with their boots. The forwards are allowed to push against their opposition to move over the ball. Gradually one side will get the ball to the back of the scrum where the scrum half can pick it up again (not an easy job for a small boy surrounded by hulking forwards) and pass it out to the back line via the fly half.

If the boys fall over on top of each other, this is called a *collapsed scrum* and if it is obviously accidental the same scrum half will put the ball in again, once the boys have all stood up and reorganised themselves into a new scrum.

A collapsed scrum

If, however, the referee considers that one team *brought down* the scrum deliberately, then he will give the ball to the opposition team to kick. In addition the ball can be given to the opposition if the ball does not go into the scrum *straight*—that is, exactly between the two hookers—or if the referee believes the scrum half is holding on to the ball for too long before putting it into the scrum. Yes, being a scrum half is a job full of responsibility—you can be justly proud if your small son has chosen this as his preferred position.

Mauls and Rucks

More mothers seem to ask, 'What's the difference between a maul and a ruck?' than almost any other question about rugby.

A *maul* occurs when the forwards gather round each other with the **ball off the ground** in their hands and try to pass it between each other. Sometimes they will even succeed in passing it out to the backs.

A *rolling maul* occurs when the forwards move out and round as the ball moves back through the maul and they rejoin the maul at the back, gradually moving forwards down the pitch towards the try line.

A *ruck* occurs when the same moving group hug seems to be taking place, but now the **ball will be down on the ground** and the forwards will push against each other (much as they do in a scrum) to push their team over the ball until it appears at the back, whereupon either the scrum half (lucky little chap) can pass it out or one of the back row forwards can pick it up and try to run with the ball again. The ball can be dropped to the ground in a maul just as long as the ball is placed behind the player who was previously holding it.

Rugby games are frequently spent with the forwards moving from maul to ruck to maul and the backs may complain that they never get to see the ball, let alone run with it. Equally the forwards will frequently complain that when they do pass the ball to the backs the latter promptly lose it to the opposition and the forwards then have to go and get it back again!

New rules relating to rucks and mauls seem to come into effect from season to season, so ask your son if you don't understand what is happening!

Backs—Their Roles and Play

The Scrum Half

We have already given you a good idea of the scrum half's role in rugby. He is the link between the forwards and the backs and is noted for his ability to throw the ball whilst horizontal a couple of feet above the ground. Of course, once he has got rid of the ball he collapses in a heap and has to scramble to his feet and keep up with the play on the field. Of all the players on the field, the scrum half probably does the most running as he dashes from one situation to the next to link forwards and backs together, and he must therefore be particularly fit.

The Fly Half
Usually one of the quickest thinkers on the pitch, the fly half is responsible for deciding whether it is worth *running the ball* by passing it down the line of backs or whether they would get farther down the pitch if he kicked the ball towards the other team and risked losing it to their backs. As a result of these options he is frequently blamed for the ball being lost to the opposition and needs great strength of character to withstand the complaints of his team when he gets the decision wrong. Of course, when he gets the decision right he can be everyone's hero!

The Centres
They line up outside the fly half and are next in line to receive the ball. If the ball is being run well towards the try line, occasionally they will pass it out to the wingers, speedy individuals (not always particularly large members of the team) who can be relied on to sprint for the line and score tries if they are not tackled by the opposition.

The Wingers
The wing three-quarters often end a game without ever touching a ball, thanks to the forwards not letting the backs see the ball and the centres not wanting to pass it out to them but preferring to dash in opposite directions across the pitch (this manoeuvre, incidentally, invariably results in the centre running into the pack of opposition forwards, getting tackled and losing the ball, much to his team mates' disgust).

The Full Back
Finally we come to the full back. As previously pointed out, he is frequently blamed for the team losing but on a good day he

can kick the ball long and hard to get his team out of trouble and sometimes sets up good running tries. The full back (especially in senior teams) is often the player who takes conversion kicks and penalty kicks.

There is another reason for a boy becoming a full back. During the initial lessons he may conclude that this position right at the back (similar to a goal keeper in Association Football) affords the best position from which to avoid any action whatsoever and keep him from getting hurt. He will eventually learn that this is not the case, but for a brief time will enjoy playing rugby without getting hurt—indeed, he will rarely touch the ball or the opposition at all.

Kicking the Ball

The ball is kicked in several situations.

1 *Conversion kicks.* When a try has been scored, the team's best kicker (usually the fly half or full back) will try to convert that try by kicking the ball over the crossbar between the posts. The ball is always placed back on the pitch exactly in line with the point where the try was scored, but the kicker can go backwards (away from the goal) as far as he wants before taking the kick, provided he remains in line with the scoring position.

2 *Penalty kicks.* These are taken whenever the opposition has broken the laws in some way (see infringements later). The kick is taken through the point where the infringement occurred and can either be taken by the ball being placed on the ground and kicked, or by the kicker holding it in his hands and dropping the ball to kick it in the air.

Penalty kicks can be taken in front of the goal posts and result in points being scored if the ball succeeds in passing through the posts in the required manner.

3 *Clearance kicks.* These can be taken at any time during the game and are normally used to improve a side's position on

the field. If the kicker is inside his own 22 metre area, then he may kick the ball directly into touch, for a line-out at that point. If he is outside this area, the ball must bounce before the side line, or the line-out has to be taken from a point level with where the ball was kicked and not where it left the pitch.

4 *Very high kicks*. These are used to allow the kicking side to catch the ball or compete for it. These are the kicks known as *up and unders* in Rugby League Football. It might seem that the backs are giving the ball to the opposition by doing this, but the poor chap trying to catch the swirling ball as it plummets towards him from the sky, whilst a horde of speeding backs charge towards him, stands no chance of catching it. The attacking team can then go on to pick up the ball and run with it again. Of course it is traditional for the full back to be the defending catcher—no wonder he lives in fear of his team mates blaming him for losing the game!

INFRINGEMENTS VARIOUS (INCLUDING DANGEROUS PLAY)

Standard Tackle

The standard accepted tackle involves one player grasping another below the waist to pull his opponent to the ground. Shirts are often torn at early levels of rugby as shirt grabbing is easier. Swinging players around by the arm can also be effective when size and weight differentials are noticeable in their early teens. Ideally, however, all tackles should take place around the waist or below. Boys will soon discover that grabbing a shirt may help to topple a running back but will rarely have any effect on a sturdy forward.

The Tap Tackle

This is a perfectly legal method of tackling a running player, by tapping the back of his feet or legs while he is running to upset his balance and trip him up. The runner is less likely to get hurt than the tackler, who risks being kicked in the face as he reaches for the speeding player's heels. Yet again, the full back is the master of this masochistic form of tackling and proudly wears the resultant black eyes.

The High Tackle

Rugby commentators on television have taught us the value of the high tackle. It flattens the best player in the opposition and prevents him from taking any further part in the game. It is of course completely illegal and, thankfully, my own sons' school takes a particularly dim view of any boy trying out this particular manoeuvre and actively discourages the boys from attempting it. Let's hope the same is true for your son.

A high tackle is one where the player grabs at his opponent's head, instead of lower down. Tall boys will complain that it is difficult to get down low enough to tackle smaller boys, but they too have to learn that a high tackle is potentially lethal. Grabbing boys by the collars of their shirts is similar and is also discouraged and can be penalised by a penalty kick being given to the opposition and, in severe cases, the offender will be sent off.

The (Accidental) Forward Pass

All passes which do not go behind the player passing are called forward passes and are illegal. They result in the ball being handed to the opposition for a scrum. All boys will tell you that such passes are accidental, and indeed at their level of competence this will probably be true!

The Hand-off

This is a useful weapon in the armoury of the older rugby players. It consists of running with the ball tucked under one arm whilst holding the other arm out, so that any unsuspecting opposition tackler will be pushed out of the way by the force of the push the player can give him. This can be likened to jousting, where the lance was held out in front of the rider so that he could topple his opponent after galloping at speed towards each other.

The hand-off

It is a perfectly legal way of resisting being tackled and has a great psychological effect on the opposition once it is perfected. The sight of a large forward (or even a back) charging at you with his arm outstretched is surely enough to put fear into the bravest of souls. The thought of having your shoulder pummelled by this speeding ramrod must be terrifying. Of course the hand-off should only be aimed at the opponent's body, never his face, and it is an important technique to learn to use with care.

Pulling Down the Scrum

Scrums can and do collapse. The group hug can rapidly turn into what seems to be a group orgy (frequently punctuated with shouts of 'watch where you're trampling' and 'mind my head'). Usually the collapse is unintentional but occasionally it is deliberate.

This is a practice which should be severely discouraged since it can result in back and neck injuries to the forwards and all boys should be taught that this practice is illegal as early as possible in their playing careers. If the referee believes the scrum has been deliberately *brought down*, he will penalise the team involved by offering their opposition a penalty kick.

All forwards should be taught that the aim of scrummaging is to push upwards against your opponents, to push them back away from the ball and enable the ball to be heeled back to the scrum half. Once good practice has been absorbed it will hopefully never be forgotten and less dangerous play will safeguard a boy's future rugby career.

Holding Onto the Ball

When tackled and brought to the floor, the ball must be released (by passing or placing it on the floor) instantaneously. If the ball is not released the team is penalised with a penalty kick being given to the opposition.

Foul Play in General

Any foul play is of course to be discouraged, and the final lesson for all rugby players to learn is to control their tempers at all times—no matter how much they believe they have been provoked. If they can learn to control their own tempers, fewer injuries and penalties will occur.

Mum's Notes

My son's position:

My son's Rugby Coach
for this season:

Points System for the current season:

A Try ☐ points

A Conversion ☐ points

A Drop Kick ☐ points

A Penalty Kick ☐ points

(We suggest you complete this in pencil—it may well change!)

The Rugby Mum

GAME SCORES

Useful at the end of the season when reports need to be handed in.

These will greatly endear your son to his Captain, who is frequently given the job of supplying such details to the sports master.

Fixture versus	Home or away	School score	Opposition score	Son's score	Comments

PART TWO

CRICKET FOR MUMS

'Keep your bat and pad together, Jenkinson,
I'm sure your father isn't paying two thousand
pounds a term to have you flashing at balls
outside off stump . . . What do you mean, "It
hurt"? Of course it hurt, it's a cricket ball, it's
supposed to hurt!'

What is Cricket?

Hopefully you will have seen cricket in some form or other, either on television or at a school playing field or local park. The pundits tell us it is synonymous with the sound of leather on willow and hot summer's days.

For most cricketing mums, however, it will always be remembered for freezing temperatures, pouring rain, damp sandwiches, tepid tea and hours and hours of sitting, waiting for something exciting to happen.

You may recognise some of the famous names from the cricketing world—Geoff Boycott, Ian Botham, Graham Gooch *et al*. However, if you have bought or been bought this book, let's assume that really you know *nothing whatsoever* about the game. If you already have some understanding I apologise for the introductory detail but hope you will find something to amuse or enlighten you on other pages.

Let me commence by apologising for referring almost exclusively to boys' cricket. I do appreciate that there are many girls playing the game these days, but since my sphere of expertise is related to boys' cricket, I will have to limit most of my comments to that branch of the sport. Nevertheless most of the details of the game apply equally to both sexes.

Let's start with a bit of history—just to set the scene.

A CRICKET HISTORY LESSON

The history of cricket is one of the vaguest pieces of historical record I have ever tried to research. I have, however, done my best to pull the basic facts from a myriad collection of sources and hope they are as accurate as possible.

According to various encyclopaedias the game is generally believed to have originated in England among shepherds using their crooks as bats, and the earliest games officially recorded were played in south-east England in the 1550s. The earliest

wickets may well have been narrow sheep-pens. Originally the bats were curved, rather like large versions of early hockey sticks (straight bats were introduced in about 1780) and until early in the nineteenth century all bowling was underarm.

There are many other wonderful suggestions for the beginnings of cricket, amongst which is a picture kept in the Bodleian Library, Oxford, depicting mediaeval monks standing in a field. One brother is bowling to another who is attempting to hit the ball with his cricce (a staff or crutch). This

Quomodo est ille!

is thought by experts to be a game of 'club-ball', a forerunner of cricket, but it could simply be a picture of some monks having a bit of a laugh in the middle of a field.

The early laws of cricket were pretty basic and included the prescribed length of the pitch (22 yards), the use of two stumps (one at each end of the pitch), underarm bowling and—at that time—four balls to an over.

There are now 42 laws in all, and many of these have clauses and sub-clauses. They cover such matters as time-wasting; umpires; substitutes; the rolling, sweeping, mowing, watering and marking of the pitch; the tea interval (very vital to cricketing mums); dead balls; and unfair play. They are very soberly written, greatly respected and occupy over thirty pages of very small print (obviously cricketers all have excellent eyesight!).

A history of cricket is kept by *Wisden*, the chronicler of the game whose annual almanac gives details of cricketing records and results of all matches played.

The first recorded match played by women was at Gosden Common, Surrey, on 26th July 1745 and around 1807 Christina Willes is said to have introduced the roundarm bowling style—said to have been necessary to avoid catching the bowling hand on the ladies' crinolines!

The birthplace of modern cricket is generally agreed to be Hambledon Club in Hampshire. Some of the club's members went on to form the White Conduit Club in the mid 1780s and this then drifted into the Marylebone Cricket Club (MCC) when the groundsman, Thomas Lord, laid the first ground in Dorset Square in London. Subsequent movements of the turf by Thomas Lord finally resulted in the establishment of Lord's Cricket Ground in St John's Wood, the current home of the MCC and Middlesex County Cricket Club.

There are many excellent books on the subject of cricket history and if your interest has been kindled by this small book, do search them out at your local library or bookshop and you will begin to see why this sport holds such a fascination for its devotees.

Terminology for Beginners

Before getting into details on the game itself, here are a few words and phrases that you will come across in this book, whose explanation might make the subsequent text slightly easier to understand.

The Playing Area

Bail(s)	Small moulded sticks placed on top of stumps at the beginning of a match.
Boundary	The edge of the playing area, marked by a white line, rope or fence.
Crease	The area in front of the wickets in which a batsman may safely bat and within which a bowler must bowl (see the plan of a pitch on p. 56).
Pitch	The 22-yard strip between the two wickets.
Stump(s)	The three long sticks which, together with the bails, form the wicket and are placed at either end of the pitch.
Wicket(s)	The stumps and bails together. Also, just to confuse the novice, the pitch between the two sets of stumps (see drawing overleaf).

Equipment

Arm-pad	A pad which straps to the forearm to protect the bones from damage.

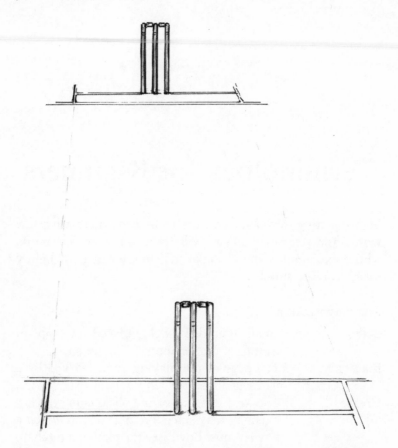

Bat   Traditionally made of willow and consisting
               of a blade with shoulder, handle and grip.
Boots   Made of white leather with a strengthened
               toe cap and metal studs in the base. Some-
               times replaced these days by lighter-weight
               trainer-type shoes with rubber studs similar
               to American football training shoes and
               called 'Pimples'. These are used in preference
               to studded shoes on harder pitches and save
               the wearer from getting sore feet from the
               studs pressing into the sole of his foot on hard
               ground.

Box	The plastic protective device for insertion in a pouch to protect vital organs against damage from bat or ball.
Cap	A hat worn by senior cricketers and awarded in special circumstances to outstanding cricketers.
Colours	A tie or other insignia awarded to members of a house or school team when they have played particularly well during a cricket season.
Gloves	Padded and specially designed to protect the hands from damage. Special gloves are used by wicket-keepers with webbing between the fingers to aid catching the ball.
Helmet	The protective head-gear now needed to protect heads from the marauding effects of very fast bowling—also used by close fielders.
Pads	Regular leg pads, worn by all batsmen and the wicket-keeper—at senior levels the wicket-keeper has specially designed pads which differ from ordinary batsman's pads.
Thigh-pad	A protective pad worn under the trousers, it fixes to the thigh that the batsman places forwards towards the bowler as he plays a stroke. Other protective pads, such as chest pads, also exist but are rarely used in junior cricket.

Players

Batsmen	Two at a time. In an ideal world the batsman facing the bowler hits the ball *every time* it is bowled correctly at him; however, it is the bowler's job to ensure that he cannot do this.
Bowlers	One at a time. Ideally the bowler would like to hit the wicket with the ball every time he bowled it! Obviously this is not the case in

reality, or else matches would be over extremely rapidly. In addition, some balls are bowled specifically to tempt the batsman to hit out in such a way that he gives a catch to the fielders.

Fielders	Ten in the field including the wicket-keeper (plus the bowler to complete the team of eleven players).
Scorer	Essential member of the team (sometimes a mum) who will keep score to ensure the result is official.
Runner	If a batsman has an injury that prevents him from running but not from batting, a runner is appointed from the batting team. To ensure he does not have an unfair advantage, he too is fully kitted out with pads, gloves and a bat.
Twelfth man	The extra player who can replace an injured member of the fielding team. To avoid accusations of cheating, the twelfth man is not normally allowed to bowl or to field in a position close to the batsman. He cannot be used as a simple substitute (as is done in football, for example).
Umpire	Two non-team people, usually one member of staff for each team in school cricket, who wear white coats and stand on the pitch and give decisions on wickets and runs, no-balls and wides and any other decisions (such as when to take tea) that may be needed during a match.
Wicket-keeper	The 'backstop' of cricket. It is his responsibility to catch the ball after it has been bowled, assuming the batsman fails to make contact in a meaningful way. In addition he is frequently able to take catches and help dismiss batsmen from the wicket.

Play

Balls/overs	The match is sub-divided into overs made up of six balls per over (that is, the bowler bowls the ball six times from one end before the ball is transferred to a different bowler at the other end of the pitch).
Bowling	The action of casting the ball forwards, with the arm held straight after wheeling it round once. A cricketer is never allowed to 'throw' the ball using a bent arm but must always 'bowl' the ball correctly.
Declaring/ declaration	Any team which believes it has scored enough runs to beat the opposition has the option of *declaring* or stopping batting. Team A can then make the other team (Team B) bat and if Team A succeeds in getting Team B out before they have overtaken Team A's score, Team A will have won the match.
Extras	Wides and no-balls give extra runs to the batting team over and above those run by the two batsmen. In both cases a single run is added to the score and an extra ball has to be bowled by the offending bowler. If, however, the batsmen run for wides and no-balls they can accumulate runs in the normal way and in this case no extra run is given. Other extras come from byes and leg byes (see the explanations later).
Innings	Each match is divided into innings (one or two for each team depending on the length of the match), which are then subdivided into overs (see above).
Lunch/Tea	A break in play is made for the two teams, plus the umpires, to eat lunch or tea and have a drink. In addition, in very hot weather, drinks

breaks are taken during the match, but in this case the teams do not leave the field of play.

Match A game of cricket between two teams; it can last for an afternoon or anything up to five days.

Wicket Taking a wicket is the term used to describe the dismissal of the batsman from the field. A batsman is said to *lose his wicket* or be *out* and he is replaced by another member of his team until all eleven have batted and ten have lost their wickets, which marks the end of that team's innings.

An Introduction
to the Game

PREPARING A FIELD FOR CRICKET

In order to prepare a field for playing cricket, the following actions need to be taken:

1   The field is mown.
2   A 'square' in the middle is mown even shorter.
3   A 'pitch' on the square 22 yards long is mown shortest of all and gives the appearance of having had all the grass completely eliminated from its surface.

Once the mowing has taken place the pitch is marked with white lines. Two white *creases* are marked at each end of the pitch. These indicate the areas from which a bowler may safely bowl, in that he must have at least part of his front foot behind the crease line at the moment he releases the ball. The crease also marks the area in which a batsman may safely stand (see *stumpings* and *run-outs* pp. 71–2).

The boundary of the field is marked either by another white line, or by a rope or fence.

Two sets of three wooden sticks called *stumps* are inserted at either end of the pitch and the umpires place two bridging pieces of wood called *bails* on both sets of stumps at the beginning of a match. These form the *wickets*.

A game of cricket begins when two batsmen from the batting team come onto the pitch and stand at either end, behind the crease and in front of the wickets. The fielding team spread themselves around the pitch. The picture below shows a typical cricket ground, marked out and with the possible fielding positions shown. For details of these see p. 57.

THE PITCH

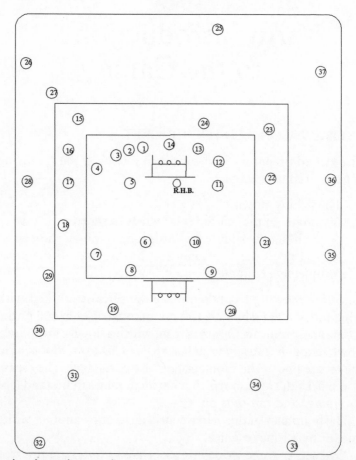

In the above diagram the centre square marks the area for close fielders, the next square out is the in-field and the remainder of the pitch is known as the out-field.
R.H.B. = Right Handed Batsman

Key

Close field	In-Field	Out-Field
1 First Slip	15 Short Third-man	25 Deep Fine-leg
2 Second Slip	16 Backward Point	26 Deep Third-man
3 Third Slip	17 Point	27 Third-man
4 Gully	18 Cover Point	28 Deep Point
5 Silly Point	19 Mid-off	29 Extra Cover
6 Silly Mid-off	20 Mid-on	30 Deep Extra
7 Short Extra	21 Mid-wicket	31 Deep Mid-off
8 Short Mid-off	22 Square-leg	32 Long-off
9 Short Mid-on	23 Backward Square-leg	33 Long-on
10 Silly Mid-on	24 Short Fine-leg	34 Deep Mid-on
11 Forward Short-leg		35 Deep Mid-Wicket
12 Backward Short-leg		36 Deep Square-leg
13 Leg-slip		37 Long-leg
14 Wicket keeper		

THE AIMS OF THE GAME

The main aims of cricket are *scoring runs* and *taking wickets*. Generally the team or *side* that scores the most runs in a match wins.

In order to score runs the batsman *on strike*—that is, facing the bowler—has to hit the ball away with his bat and then run the length of the pitch, crossing over with his fellow batsman *en route*. Each time the batsmen cross and reach the safe area behind the crease at the opposite end, a run is scored.

If the ball crosses the boundary either at ground level or having bounced on the pitch, four runs are scored. The batsmen do not have to run and cross over in order for this to occur. If the ball crosses the boundary without touching the ground after leaving the batsman's bat it will score six runs. With this additional scoring ability it is possible to score 36 runs in one over—but this has rarely been achieved and certainly never at schoolboy level to the author's knowledge.

Runs are also scored even when the ball has not been hit by the bat. If the fielders do not retrieve the ball immediately and the batsmen manage to run the length of the wicket they can add runs. If the ball has glanced off any part of the batsman other than his bat or glove these runs are called *leg byes*, even if the ball hits the batsman's head! If the ball has not touched the batsman at all he can still run and these runs will be *byes*.

It is not unusual in schools cricket for a fast bowler to defeat not only the batsman but also his wicket-keeper and for four byes to be awarded to the batting team as the ball speeds towards and over the boundary without anyone touching it. Whilst this demonstrates the speed of the fast bowler it does nothing for his credibility as a team player and he will often be ticked off by his team mates for bowling too fast and not straight enough!

In addition, if the fielders throwing back the ball to the wickets aim badly and neither the bowler nor the wicket-keeper is able to stop the ball, *overthrows* occur and the batsmen can continue to run until the ball is returned to the wicket area.

There are two other ways in which runs can be scored by the batting side:

1 *No balls* occur when the bowler oversteps the crease while delivering the ball. The umpire is supposed to shout 'No ball' clearly and stick an arm out sideways so that the batsman knows he may take a mighty swing at the ball, since the only way you can be out (or lose your wicket) off a no ball is to be *run out* (unless the batsman hits the ball twice or obstructs the fielders, both of which would result in his summary dismissal).

2 *Wides* are balls bowled so wide of the wicket that a batsman couldn't reasonably be expected to hit them, even if he wanted to.

Both faulty bowling deliveries result in one run being allotted to the batting team: if the batsman uses his bat and running energy then he can score more than one run and the *extra* run is not recorded on his score. However, the bowler has to bowl extra balls in that over to compensate and it is not unheard of for 10 or 12 balls to be bowled in an over at school level (which makes the scorer's job extra hard).

At the end of the team's innings, the total number of runs scored is added up. The other team has to get at least one run more before losing ten wickets. If both teams score the same number of runs the match is a tie, and (in limited overs only) the side losing fewer wickets is the winner.

In senior cricket there is another possibility, a draw, but for schools cricket this will only apply if the match is not a limited over match. In such matches the result can be a draw if the side batting second does not pass the total of the other side but has not lost all its wickets at the close of play.

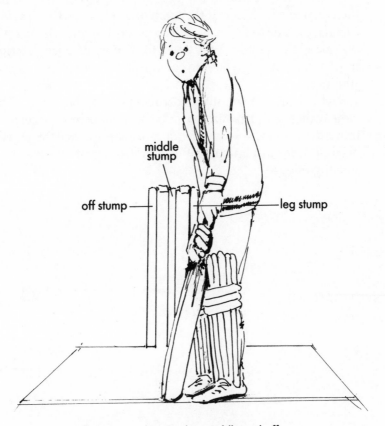

middle
stump

off stump —————   ————— leg stump

The stumps, showing leg, middle and off

The stumps (which play an essential part in the game) are given specific names. A right-handed batsman usually stands to face a right-handed bowler with his body placed in such a position that either his body or bat are in front of the *leg* stump.

The pitch (see p. 56) is divided into an *on* (leg) side and an *off* side. Thus fielding positions are given names associated with their position on the field and mid-off, mid-on, etc., exist with long-leg, short-leg, etc. The on and off locations are shown with reference to a right-handed batsman, who would stand ready to bat with his left shoulder towards the bowler. The resultant position of his legs in relation to the bat would then dictate which side of the pitch becomes the leg or *on* side (that is, the side to which he will naturally hit) and which is the *off* side of the pitch. See pp. 80–4 for a more detailed description of the major positions in the field and their responsibilities.

Well, that's a very short introduction to the game. Obviously there is much more to it than this but before we get into more details let's discuss the kit your son (or daughter) will need in order to play the game at school when he (or she) is starting out.

Equipment Needed to Play Cricket

In the early stages children can play cricket in their school sports kit of shorts, a T-shirt and a pair of trainers. However, once they start to play matches, or for longer periods than a games lesson, it will be preferable if they have long trousers to protect their legs and prevent chafing from the pads they will need to wear when they bat. Although initially they will use a tennis ball or soft ball, once a real cricket ball is used they will have to wear pads and box to protect themselves.

Keen cricketing boys, however, will insist on having all their own kit straight away. This can be a very expensive experience and will probably require the following purchases:

1 short-sleeved shirt and/or 1 long-sleeved shirt
1 long-sleeved sweater (preferably in school colours—this of course makes it more expensive!) and/or 1 sleeveless sweater
1 pair of cricket boots/shoes (with strengthened toe caps—optional)
1 pair cricket trousers
1 pair white socks
1 bat
1 set of pads
1 pair gloves
1 cap

and last but not least 1 cricketer's protective box (and jock-
strap or pouch)—for boys only

This should set up even the keenest boys for their first year of
cricket, but as the years go by additional specialised boots,
extra shirts, socks, trousers and so on will be needed to cope
with practices, matches and games lessons, all within a few
days of each other. Girls generally seem to continue to wear
divided skirts and trainers despite the chafing of the pad straps
and the hard balls—so which is the harder sex?

As a cricketing mother your role in all this is obvious. It will
be up to you to restrain your small son from buying equipment
that is a) too large, b) too heavy and c) too expensive! He will
have little idea what size bat to buy and will often choose one
that is too heavy for a long batting innings. Although he will
grow rapidly and the weight will lessen in proportion, many a
lad returns home from his first cricket match with aching arms,
having swung his new bat around for longer than he expected
and worn himself out completely.

The desire to possess the most expensive bat in the rack, or
the most expensive pair of pads, seems irresistible to small
boys—like the need for designer names on jeans and trainers.
However, a sensible mother will resist such requests and only
purchase reasonably priced kit, since there is no guarantee that
her son will pursue a cricketing career past the first few years
and such expense can rarely be recouped in full—although
part can be recovered by selling on his kit to younger pupils
through the school second-hand uniform shop (if your school
is lucky enough to have one).

The most embarrassing part of the kit is of course the *box*.
This protective piece of plastic is essential once the boys are
playing serious cricket, but the advice of your friendly shop-
keeper will allay your son's fears when he is required to decide
what size box he requires. Since he will probably not replace
this item until he is old enough to go shopping alone, the initial
purchase should allow for a certain amount of growth. The
addition of a jock strap to contain the box may also be

required, but this can be omitted if the embarrassment factor for your son is too great and a pair of tight-fitting underpants will do the job just as well.

However as his career develops, if he becomes a regular member of the school sides, his need for protective kit will increase. He will not only require his own batting pads and gloves, but also arm protective pads and thigh pads. American football this is not, but the protective kit also includes chest pads and helmets these days.

Your small son is unlikely to need a helmet unless he has a particular facial feature to protect (such as a fragile nose) or unless he is regularly facing fast bowlers who are capable of hitting him around the head. Some parents will purchase these very expensive helmets thinking their sons will wear the protective equipment at all times, but the need to be macho remains a part of a cricketer's life to this day and it is therefore only the vulnerable boys who wear a helmet from a very early age. The wearing of helmets is, however, becoming increasingly common and, if your son is good enough to represent his county, a helmet will be needed soon after he is 12 years old.

The average players will wear their school cricketing cap (if such a thing exists) or their favourite basketball cap. The addition of the white broad-brimmed hat to the Australian game to counteract sun-stroke has led to its introduction in this country, and these hats, which can be purchased at sports shops and cricket grounds, are often found decorating the heads of junior players during the summer months. Test cricketers have also taken to wearing ski-style gold-mirrored sun glasses recently and your son may consider it *de rigeur* to wear similar glasses whilst fielding. These come at vast expense from the USA but can, I have found, be replicated very cheaply at your local bike shop!

A final thought: the whole idea of wearing *whites* for cricket must have been invented by a man, since any self-respecting housewife would have immediately pointed out the total impracticality of choosing such a colour for playing a game in

Mum's role is to restrain her son from buying kit that is too large, too heavy and too expensive.

which boys and men regularly throw themselves around on muddy and grassy fields, and it should be noted that the wearing of whites was not compulsory until the late 1800s.

Playing a Game

So now your son has the clothes, what about playing a game?

There is a wonderful introduction to cricket which is printed on tea towels and other collectables. It goes something like this:

> There are two teams of eleven players.
>
> One team goes in to bat and the other team stays out in the field.
>
> Two batsmen from the team that is in go out to bat.
>
> The rest of the team that is in stay out in the pavilion until one of their team is out, then he is replaced by another member of the team who is sitting out waiting his turn to go in to bat.
>
> This is continued until all the team that are in are out.
>
> Then the other team go in to bat and the team that were in go out to field.
>
> When both teams have been in and out the match is over.

Obviously this is very misleading, not to mention mind-blowingly confusing. So let's give it another go, using some of the same terminology that you will hear during cricket commentary on radio and television, but explaining it in a little more detail.

There are indeed two teams of eleven players, but there is also a *twelfth man* in each team. As explained earlier, if a player is injured during a match, the twelfth man is allowed to replace him as a fielder. He is not allowed to bowl or field close in but can help keep the team complete by fielding in the outfield. However, he cannot bat when his team goes in.

At schools level the twelfth man is often a less able cricketer than the rest of the team, since if he was capable he would either be one of the original eleven or be in the school B team. He is frequently brought along for his ability to keep score (cricket score books are notoriously complicated) and sometimes for his ability to supply extra food and water to his team mates.

The only time when the twelfth man is of equal skill to his team mates is when the team is playing in a Cup match. There are several major competitions for schools—amongst which are the regional NatWest competitions. When playing this type of game the reserve player needs to be as skilled as his peers since he will play in the event of an injury to one of them. Even so he rarely gets to play, but he can nevertheless take pleasure in just being part of a winning team.

The components of a cricket match vary at different levels, but since this is an introduction for mums, let's assume your son (or daughter) will be playing a variety of *limited-over cricket*.

LIMITED-OVER CRICKET

All cricket matches are divided into two halves or *innings*. However, these two sections are not always equal halves in terms of time. The innings are then subdivided into *overs*. The overs are limited to a set number in each innings to create a limited-over match.

Before the game can commence the two captains meet to toss a coin to decide which team will bat first.

There are two umpires for cricket games (usually at schools level it will be a master from each of the schools involved), but if you watch Test cricket on television these days, you will hear reference to the *third umpire*. This person remains indoors throughout the match, seated in front of a television screen on which he can watch slow-motion action replays of key moments in the match, such as when a batsman might be *run out* (I will explain this term later).

Once the toss has taken place, the team that have chosen to bat (or have been *put in* to bat by their opposition) will leave the field and settle themselves down near the pavilion. Two of them will put on pads and other protective kit and go out to the wicket to start their team's innings.

The other team will spread their eleven players around the pitch and two of their number will have a specific role. One is the *wicket-keeper*—this is the lad wearing cricket pads and gloves who stands behind the stumps. His pads and gloves are specially designed versions and differ from those worn by batsmen in certain ways. The gloves are generally larger and may have webbing between the fingers, for instance.

It is the wicket-keeper's job to stop the ball that has been bowled by the bowler from going too far past the stumps. If he performs his role well he can save his team mates considerable time and energy by preventing the need for players to chase balls which have been bowled past the batsman. In addition the wicket-keeper catches balls that glance off the bat, and guards the stumps to ensure that balls being thrown in from the field do not go past the wicket.

Young wicket-keepers, however, have generally not yet honed their skills sufficiently to cope with the vagaries of their peers' bowling techniques (in other words the bowlers cannot yet bowl in a straight line at a regular point on the pitch). As a result, many badly bowled balls will evade the wicket-keeper's grasp and have to be chased by his team mates down to the boundary (especially when a young fast bowler is at work).

The other specialists in the fielding team are the bowlers. In the next chapter you will find a description of the various types of bowler which I hope you will find useful. They are usually described according to the speed with which they attack the opposition—fast, slow, medium and so on—but there are various other descriptions which are obviously designed to baffle the average cricketing mum.

A wide

The bowler bowls the ball to a batsman in set periods called *overs*. Each over consists of six balls being bowled to one end of the wicket. Once the six balls have been bowled, the bowling *changes ends* and another bowler *comes on* to bowl from the opposite end of the wicket. This means that if a batsman does not succeed in scoring any runs during a particular over he will not have to face the next six balls. Equally, if a very good batsman is playing with a poorer player he can attempt to score an odd number of runs in an over to ensure that he faces the different bowler during the next over.

Sometimes you will notice that more than six balls are

bowled during an over. This is because *no balls* or *wides* have been called by the umpires and extra balls are bowled to make up for this.

As I explained above, in *limited-over cricket* the maximum number of overs each team is allowed to bowl is set beforehand, between thirty and forty being about the right number for an afternoon match. Once both teams have batted for the same number of overs the scores are compared and the team with the highest number of runs wins the match. If the runs are even then the team with the least number of wickets lost will win. So two teams scoring 120 runs but one with a score of 120 for 7 (seven wickets lost) will win compared with the other team with a score of 120 for 9.

Usually, for an afternoon school cricket match, another method of limiting the overs is used: it may be agreed that the match will finish 20 overs after, say, six o'clock. The umpires and the scorers will make a note when six o'clock occurs and count the number of overs after that time, and will warn the teams when they are approaching their final overs.

Schools cricket that is played in this way, without strictly limited overs, can be very tedious and is often a frustrating experience. If the first team to bat are not scoring particularly fast, they can stay at the *crease* until their captain is happy they have scored enough runs to give them a chance of beating the opposition. He will also aim to give the opposition insufficient time to beat his team!

As a result the first team may stay in from 2.00 p.m. and continue *after* the tea break, which is usually taken around 4.15 p.m. If they declare after five o'clock this can leave the opposition with only just over an hour of batting time compared with up to three hours used by the first team—not a fair match at all and definitely not cricket!

GETTING OUT, OR LOSING A WICKET

There are several ways in which a batsman can be out or *lose his wicket*.

The first is being *bowled out*. The bowler succeeds in getting the ball past the batsman and it knocks the bails off the stumps.

If this happens the fielders will rush over to congratulate the bowler and pat him on the back whilst the dejected batsman makes his way back to the pavilion, to be replaced by another member of his team. As the batsmen pass, words are frequently exchanged with the departing player, giving his team member guidance on how to avoid a similar fate when playing against that particular bowler.

The second way to lose a wicket, and the simplest to appreciate, is being *caught out*. The batsman hits the ball into the air and one of the fielders catches it.

At this point all the fielders standing close by rush towards the fielder who has caught the ball and congratulate him, especially the bowler who gets the wicket credited to his name, too. The kissing and hugging of football players is not encouraged, but pats on the back and hugs are seen, as well as much American-style clapping of two players' hands together in a salute—the fact that they look as if they are playing pat-a-cake is entirely incidental.

The third, and most controversial, way of losing a wicket, is being out *leg before wicket*. In order for a batsman to be out *leg before*, the ball must strike the batsman anywhere except on his bat or gloves, in such a way that if the ball had continued to travel through without interference, it would have knocked the bails off the stumps.

The batsman is much less likely to be out *leg before wicket* if he has moved well forward in his stroke play and his front foot (the foot placed farthest towards the other end of the wicket) is well outside the crease. The decision process involved in ensuring that a player is fairly given 'out LBW' is far too complicated for an instant explanation here. Suffice it to say that there are many good books (including cricket's own rule book) which will explain the detail to you if you are interested.

The one absolute requirement for an LBW decision to be taken is that a member of the fielding team (often the bowler) should shout loudly, 'Howzzat!' (or How was that?) to the umpire to claim the wicket. This is called making an appeal.

At the very early stages of cricket (such as the first proper match) it is not unheard-of for a young team to get a player out LBW but not know to appeal, and therefore the batsman gets to remain at the crease. Needless to say they learn this lesson extremely rapidly and soon shouts of 'Howzzat' will resound around the field at regular intervals whether the batsman could be out or not.

Generally the players will not rush to congratulate the bowler immediately on an LBW decision, since they have to wait for the umpire to declare the batsman 'out'. The umpire signifies this by raising his index finger to shoulder level and pointing his hand skywards, a little like a teacher wagging his finger at a naughty boy. Once the decision has been taken, however, the bowler will receive the usual plaudits from his fellow team members.

It is frequently difficult for the umpire to tell exactly whether or not the ball would have hit the stumps, and at schools level they will tend to be lenient (especially, it sometimes seems, to their own team!). This will be the first experience the boys get of the inequities of umpiring and it takes great strength of character on their part not to object too vociferously if they believe the batsman should have been out.

This leads to much under the breath muttering from the fielders and shaking of heads. Comments on the quality of the umpire's eyesight and his need for a visit to the nearest optician should, however, be avoided. Good teaching staff will always be fair to both sides and it is hoped that the boys will learn to accept all umpires' decisions accordingly. The umpire is only human (despite some of the comments which you may hear after a match) and he can be right and wrong in equal measure. Learning to accept his decision as final with good grace is another part of the character-building nature of team sport which we should seek to encourage in our youngsters.

The fourth way a batsman can be out is to be *stumped*. If the batsman strays outside the crease in front of his stumps,

The umpire signals 'out'

because he has just tried to hit the ball, the wicket-keeper can knock the bails off the stumps with the ball and the batsman will be out if he is outside the crease at the moment the bails are removed. The umpire standing at square leg (see diagram, p. 56) is responsible for making this decision.

The fifth way a batsman can be out is to be *run out*. In order to score runs the batsmen are required to change ends and run down the wicket between the two sets of stumps. Once their bat or any part of their body touches the ground inside the crease at the opposite end they cannot be run out.

However, if they are in the middle of the wicket and the bails are knocked from the stumps, either by the wicket-keeper or another player with the ball in his hands, or directly by the ball being thrown by a fielder at the stumps, then the stranded batsman nearest those stumps will be out.

The batsman cannot be out if either a foot or his bat are on the ground inside the line of the crease. For this reason you will often see boys going through major contortions as they prepare to run down the pitch, with their body facing forwards and legs set to sprint but their batting arm stretched behind their back with the bat placed firmly on the ground behind them.

When batsmen are about to run it is usually up to the one who can see the direction of the ball best to call out to say if the run will be safe or not. If his opposite number countermands this call he must do so immediately and firmly, otherwise one of the batsmen will set off down the pitch and will risk being run out. The normal calls are 'yes' or 'no'. However, if the decision can't be made until later—perhaps depending on the efficiency of a fielder—the initial call will be 'wait' or 'waiting' and once the fielder's action is clear this will be followed by a call of 'yes' or 'no'.

Because it is very difficult for the umpires to tell if the batsman has reached the crease before the ball hits the stumps, run-outs and stumpings are often controversial, and it is for this reason that international cricket has brought in the *third umpire*. At schools level, however, umpires will sometimes be accused of getting the decision wrong by the players from the batting team who have the benefit of a good view from the edge of the pitch.

Nevertheless, as we have previously explained, in common with all other team sports, the umpire's decision is final and all boys are trained to leave the wicket immediately they have been told by the umpire they are out—without argument or dissent. It should be noted that in the case of any doubt it is the umpire's responsibility to give the benefit of the doubt to the batsman, not the bowler.

If your son is a cricketer he will learn to play as part of a team, to help his team mates, to accept decisions from umpires—even when they are incorrect—and all these things can be taken into adulthood as useful tools. He will also learn to accept blame when he misses the wicket with a bad throw or when he loses his wicket on the first ball of his innings, and will become a stronger, more self-confident person as a result.

Finally, there are a few other ways in which a batsman can get out which are extremely rare, although you should be aware that they exist.

If the batsman himself hits the wicket, either with bat or body, and the bails are dislodged, then he will be out. This can happen when a batsman has unbalanced himself, usually playing off the back foot, and topples backwards towards the wicket. Occasionally you will see batsmen trying to leap over the stumps rather than hit them, but since high jumping or hurdling are not an integral part of cricket training, they are not usually successful in clearing the wicket in this way and are frequently out. Very occasionally it can happen, if the batsman is standing close to the wicket and his backlift of his bat is too great, that he hits the wicket with his bat as he aims for a hefty shot. Once again he is out.

If a batsman hits the ball twice he will be dismissed. This may happen if a batsman has hit the ball and sees it still continuing towards the wicket, so hits it again. He is probably aware that he will be out anyway if the ball succeeds in hitting the wicket, so his extra tap at the ball will not change the result. However, a junior batsman might automatically hit the ball to clear it back to the fielders, as he would in practice sessions, and this would result in him losing his wicket if he had already hit the ball once.

Another way a batsman can be dismissed is if he obstructs the fielding team. If he deliberately prevents a fielder from getting to the ball or throwing it at the stumps, he is deemed to be obstructing the field and will be given out. He can also be out if he picks the ball up to give it back to the other side, if he has not asked their permission to do this first.

And last of all, a batsman can be 'timed out' if he is believed to be spending too long preparing himself to face the attacking bowler. This is a very unusual law and is unlikely to be applied at schools level.

I hope you now have a feel for the main elements which make up a cricket match, so let me give you a bit more detail on the individual skills involved in making a first class cricket team.

The Players and Their Skills

BOWLERS

As I mentioned earlier, bowlers are frequently described by their speed in bowling the ball.

The fastest are called *fast bowlers*. At international level you will probably have heard of Fred Trueman, Devon Malcolm, or Imran Khan. The fast bowler has to be very fit, since he not only has the longest *run up* of all the bowlers but he also delivers the ball much faster than the others. This requires speed from the run up being combined with a very fast over-arm action as his bowling arm windmills round prior to bowling the ball down the wicket at the batsman. The top flight bowlers are capable of bowling the ball at over 90 mph!

Obviously schoolboys will not attain such speeds, but by their senior years the fastest are getting close to this and are duly feared by their opposition.

Then come the *medium fast bowlers*—Ian Botham was probably the best known exponent of medium fast bowling ever. They use almost as long a run up as the fast bowlers but do not have the same fast arm action.

Famous *medium pace bowlers* include England's Graham Gooch. They use a shorter run up but are still capable of bowling a good fast ball with either swing or seam affecting

Fast bowler in action

the trajectory of the ball. In addition they can achieve a greater control over the flight of the ball than their fast counterparts.

Bowlers are capable of using the seam that binds the leather ball to adjust the way the ball travels through the air or bounces off the ground. The application of shine to one side of the ball, whilst leaving the other side matt or even rough, will make the ball swing in the air, especially when the weather conditions are right. This is called *swing bowling* and at its very best it results in the ball travelling through the air with a trajectory which looks very similar to the 'banana' shot of the footballer.

Equally, if the bowler can manage to bowl the ball in such a way that it lands on the seam when it hits the ground, this will deviate the ball in one direction or another: this is called *seam bowling*.

In order to improve the ball's chances of moving sideways,

you will frequently see bowlers rubbing the ball on their trousers. Pity the mother whose son discovers this activity early in his career, since the red dye on the leather cricket balls is only too happy to transfer itself to the trousers which will then need extra treatment to return them to their former pristine glory.

You may have been aware of 'ball tampering' scandals in recent years. Once you understand the advantages of one shiny surface and one matt it is easier to comprehend why the powers-that-be in cricket get so het up over such incidents.

Medium/slow pace bowlers can vary the pace at which they bowl the ball, sometimes bowling it slowly and other times speeding up the action of their arm to bowl closer to medium pace. They usually take only a short run up and can therefore get through more overs per hour than the fast bowler who has to walk the long trek back down the pitch to reach the beginning of his run up.

In addition to the use of swing and seam there are slow bowlers called *spinners*. They have the ability to spin the ball as it flies through the air, so that when it bounces off the pitch near the batsman it goes off at an oblique angle and does not continue in a straight line, except when bowling top-spin.

This is how slow bowlers are capable of taking wickets, since the batsman can easily see the ball coming but cannot predict its trajectory after it hits the ground. All spinners use a special grip on the ball in order to persuade it to change direction. To persuade the ball to *break* or move from the off side towards the leg side one specific grip is used—generating off-spin; this is called an off-break and different grips are used to create leg-spin, top-spin and so on. The leg-spinner has an additional ball called a 'googly', which is an off-break ball bowled with a leg-break action.

Understand all this if you dare. All you need to know is that if your small son is a slow bowler, he will not just be throwing the ball down the pitch (indeed throwing the ball with a bent arm results in a no-ball being called) but will be applying every law of science he can muster to bamboozle the batsman at the opposite end of the wicket.

Is it any wonder that early bowling skills are somewhat haphazard? The slow bowlers can rarely get into too much trouble at the outset. They have to learn to bowl the full length of the wicket (farther for a four-foot eight-year-old than it seems to an adult), and they also need to learn how to bowl in a straight line on a regular basis (not as easy as it sounds with the overarm action), but once they have mastered this they can then add the use of spin to their repertoire.

Fast bowlers, however, can get into all sorts of trouble, as I have already indicated. They take longer to learn to bowl at the same place every time—given the fast run up and fast overarm action required, this is not surprising. In addition, because of the long run up they have difficulty in not over-stepping the crease as they bowl and are responsible for more 'no-ball' calls than their slower counterparts. In the early stages of a fast bowler's career he will be the chap who ends up bowling more than six balls an over regularly and will get removed from the bowling attack if he cannot get his run up right after a couple of overs.

Regrettably, it can take three or four overs for him to adjust his run up, and the captain's frustration at the extra runs being awarded to the opposition can frequently prevent the fast bowler from getting it right several matches in a row as his captain gives him his chance but only for two or three overs. The habit of using nets for bowling practice rather than the proper wicket does not help this problem, and fast bowlers frequently complain that they never get a chance to establish what their run up is in a match situation before the season actually starts.

A recent addition to the fast bowler's armoury has been the introduction of zinc-based creams to protect the players from sunburn. Facial adornments have been part of cricket ever since W. G. Grace and his famous whiskers took to the field, but inferior versions such as Mervyn Hughes' moustache and Bob Willis' 70s mop of hair have been surpassed by the recent

war paint applied by young cricketers such as Shane Warne of Australia.

I hope this has helped to clarify in your mind what it is that bowlers do and has not confused you too greatly. Now let's move on to the fielders and their role in the game.

FIELDING POSITIONS

This must be the most confusing part of cricket. It is certainly the aspect that must take the boys and girls the longest to learn, for *placing a field* is a skill that many captains even at senior level seem to struggle with—doing a good job at junior level must be even harder, especially when your team mates don't even know where the positions you want them to stand in are located. This results in a great deal of arm waving and finger pointing until the fielders take up the correct positions on the field.

Look at the diagram on p. 56 for the exact placing of

fielders. The field is divided into three areas—the close field, close to the batsman; the in-field, the next level away from the batsman; and the out-field, the area near the boundary.

Slips (first, second and third, etc.)
In theory there is no limit to the number of slip fielders you can place—however, putting in more than three would be self-defeating as this would leave the rest of the field bereft of fielders and the batsman would soon score vast numbers of runs.

The job of the slip fielders is to catch balls which just catch the bat and 'slip' off towards the off side (these are usually called *snicks* or *edges*). The slips are usually thought of as great heroes since it is their spectacular diving catches which frequently dismiss some of the best batsmen; however, their positions close up to the batsman can also be considered very dangerous and require courageous chaps to fill them. There is also a *leg slip* on the other side of the wicket (see p. 56 and 83).

Gully
This has nothing to do with being close to the area where sea-gulls land, although they frequent cricket pitches around the country and can cause problems. It is a position in line with the slips but slightly farther away from the wicket. The gully fielder is placed here to catch difficult edge and bat shoulder-height catches. If your small son fields here he must be a) a good catcher of a speeding cricket ball and b) remarkably brave!

Mid-wicket and cover point
Pretty dangerous places to stand—at a central point between the two sets of stumps where many balls are hit, some with great ferocity. They are usually responsible for running out more batsmen than all the other fielders put together.

Long-leg
Nothing to do with the size of the fielder or the length of his leg. Merely a description for a position to one side of the

batsman (on the side of leg stump) the 'long' referring to the distance from the stumps. In other words, he stands very close to the boundary. Other boundary positions have the added word *deep* to indicate their position (for example, deep third-man).

Short-leg

Long-leg

Short-leg
No, he's not the shortest boy in the team, just one of the brave ones and stands on the same line from the wicket as long leg but closer in. This is another of the hero positions of the close field.

Fine-leg

Nothing to do with Chippendale furniture or male models, this position is found between square-leg and the line of the wickets. It comes in various forms, short fine-leg, deep fine-leg but closest in it is usually called leg slip.

Silly mid-on

Given this name for a perfectly good reason—anyone in his right mind would never stand there. One good whack from the batsman could send the ball hurtling towards him at a frightening speed and could cause irreparable damage to any part of the anatomy that is hit.

Silly mid-off

Exactly the same position on the other side of the batsman— slightly less dangerous but not a lot! There are several other 'silly' positions.

You will be pleased to find out that there are special laws preventing young players (those under 14 years of age) from standing too close to the batsman because of the danger involved. Whilst this will prevent your young son or daughter from getting a serious injury early in their playing career, as soon as they get into a more senior team in the school this caution will discontinue and the 'danger positions' will become part of playing the game.

Square-leg

Again, nothing at all to do with the shape of the fielder's leg: he is merely standing on the leg side (the side of leg stump) at right angles to the length of the pitch and in line with the batsman's stumps.

Third-man

Not a Graham Greene character but a fielder who stands near the off side boundary (deep third-man standing next to the boundary rope or fence). The position is located behind and to the side of the off stump.

Square-leg

Other positions which you can discover include backward square-leg (*not* the least intelligent member of the team), short point and silly point (*not* related to horse riding, dogs or hairstyles) and short extra cover (*not* another name for a short twelfth man).

BATTING TECHNIQUES

For the purposes of these explanations I shall assume the batsman is right-handed—obviously for a left-handed player all the shots will be reversed.

When the ball is hit the batsman has hopefully raised his bat behind him (using *backlift*) prior to swinging it at the ball. If he hits hard and the bat continues on its way, it will *follow through* until it is raised above his head, forming a complete *stroke* (except when making a hook shot or check drive—see below.

Here are a few names of strokes which you will hear during cricket commentaries. This is by no means a full list, but will give you a feel for the sort of strokes used by batsmen.

Hook. Hitting the ball so that it flies off to the left, sometimes behind the batsman, to the *on* side of the field. Usually it is hit off a short-pitched ball with very little follow through of the bat.

Drive. An attacking forward stroke which comes in a variety of flavours: the cover drive, the on drive, the off drive, the check drive (not a Scot's plaid but a swing of the bat which is checked before the full follow through). It is usually hit off a full or an over-pitched ball.

Forward defensive. The *raison d'être* of Geoffrey Boycott. No one has ever played the forward defensive quite so effectively or for so long in a match as the famous Mr Boycott. It has to be the most boring shot ever invented—in fact calling it a shot is a complete misnomer, stroke is a much better description.

It consists of placing the bat with the toe of the blade firmly planted in front of the pad and the handle held forward at an angle over the blade. This results in any ball that hits the bat being immediately stopped in its tracks and returned down the pitch towards the bowler at ground level. Although boring, it is a very useful stroke for the new batsman to the crease until he gets his eye in.

The forward defensive stroke

Whilst it may prove a frustration to bowlers, who may be tempted to bowl some wild balls to make the batsman change his tactic, over after over of forward defensive play will also tend to elicit a slow hand-clapping from a modern crowd weaned on the excitement of one-day cricket and unaware of the psychological battle involved in a five-day Test match.

The forward defensive can also be played with the bat off the ground but at the identical angle. This copes with higher bouncing balls in an equally efficient (and boring) manner.

Playing off the front foot. A term to describe how the batsman is holding his body whilst batting. Generally if you bat off the front foot you will be an aggressive, pro-active batsman. The front foot is, fairly obviously, the foot placed farthest down the pitch and pushed forward to balance the body while the arms swing the bat. Batsmen normally play off the front foot for full or over-pitched balls and off the back foot for short-pitched balls.

You will frequently hear commentators on TV and radio complaining, 'He's not moving his feet.' This criticism is because the best batsmen move their feet to adjust their body position to play a shot and non-movement of the feet can indicate a nervous, reticent or incompetent batsman.

Playing off the back foot. The reverse of playing off the front foot and sometimes the sign of an unsettled batsman. The junior batsman is not well balanced when playing off the back foot and is usually playing defensively. Bowlers, fast ones especially, take great delight in bowling balls in order to force the batsman to play off the back foot. It is, however, a technique which can be mastered, and many a fast bowler has been smashed all over the ground by a quality player such as Ian Botham playing off his back foot.

Smashing it over the top. Everybody's favourite shot—both cricketer and crowd. The batsman needs to hit the ball as hard as possible and as high as possible to make sure it clears the fielders and hopefully scores either four or preferably six. The 'over the top' refers to going over the top of the in-field to clear the close fielders before reaching the boundary—hopefully without interception.

Tickle. When the batsman just touches the ball and it runs off—usually towards the leg side fielders.

Fine cut. This is a stroke played behind point (see p. 56 for this position) on the off side.

Square cut. A ball hit square on the off side.

An edge. Generally a bad shot but sometimes a lucky one—the batsman really did not hit the ball where he intended and it came off the edge of the bat. This frequently results in the batsman being caught out. Edges can be *thick* or *thin* depending on how badly the batsman missed! Occasionally, however, they can work to the batsman's advantage and send the ball off from a fast bowler at an odd angle which defeats the fielders.

Mum's Work

As a cricket mum you may have several responsibilities.

Cleaning Kit

First and foremost your son will need clean kit for every match. Sports masters have conspired over the years to ensure that mothers have as little time as possible to prepare kit and they usually organise practices at school for the evening before a match. This means if your son only has one set of kit and is a bowler who rubs the red ball on his trousers, or a fielder who dives around in the grass and mud, you will need to get his kit washed and pressed overnight. This test of your ingenuity rapidly leads you into purchasing a spare set of kit (sometimes a second-hand set) which your son can use for practices, keeping his clean good set for matches.

Years of cleaning muddy, grass-stained kit have taught us cricketing mums that there are several useful tips.

Trousers, shirts, etc.

Spray, coat or soak stains with a good proprietary stain remover (such as Vanish) prior to washing in a medium-hot wash with a powder with a bleaching action such as Daz. This will result in almost all stains being removed from the white/cream cricketer's kit.

Boots

Boots can be scrubbed with kitchen cream cleanser (Jif, Ajax, etc.) and then whitened with tennis shoe whitener. Studs will rust if left covered with mud for too long, I'm afraid, but will respond quite well to a brisk rub with a scouring pad!

Sweaters

The majority of school sweaters are made from acrylic these days and are really easy to put through a cool machine wash. They rarely pick up the same level of grass stains as the other kit and are pretty easy to care for.

However, if your son has acquired his father's old cricketing sweater—beware. It may well be wool and one machine wash will turn your husband's pride and joy into a shrunken, matted sweater at least three sizes smaller than it was. This will not only annoy your son who will not have a sweater on what you can almost guarantee will be the coldest day of the summer term, but is likely to cause your husband a great deal of anguish, too.

Woollen sweater—before and after

Cricket Teas

Since cricket first began the reputation of a club has rested on the quality of its tea. So it is for schools. The schools that can supply not just the players, but also the spectactors with an impressive tea will always be fondly remembered.

Some schools are able to use their catering facilities to supply sandwiches and cakes, but other smaller establishments will have to rely on team mothers to supply and make the tea. Favourites are fairy cakes, strawberry and chocolate sponges and of course the ubiquitous cucumber sandwich. The boys will usually devour the cakes in preference to any sandwiches supplied, whilst the spectators reverse this procedure.

Organising team cricket teas can be a thankless task. If your small son has volunteered you for this year's job, try not to strangle him just yet.

It helps to have a list of home telephone numbers of all the members of the team, so that you can contact parents and persuade them to help. Remember there will always be one or two keen cricket watchers who can be relied on to turn up to most home matches; make friends with these good souls and many of your problems will vanish since they will nearly always be there to help serve the tea, even if they have not helped to prepare the cakes and so on.

Mums who cannot make it to the match can still usually be persuaded to bake or buy one cake a term and send it in with their son on the morning of a match. Games masters are usually very amenable when it comes to collecting such offerings, but beware games masters with a sweet tooth or you may not have much cake left to offer guests by the time the tea interval occurs!

MUM'S ESSENTIAL EQUIPMENT

As a cricketing mum you will rapidly discover that you cannot just turn up to a match in your usual smart clothing and expect to enjoy an afternoon in the sun. Regrettably, the English weather is no respecter of our national summer game and regularly sends wind, rain and even hail to interrupt proceedings.

Below is a list of items which every cricketing mother will find useful and from which you can select your own favourites once you have watched a few matches.

1 A *light-weight garden chair*. Cricket pitches are usually equipped with a bench or two and some schools boast superb pavilions with balconies and viewing areas, but these are few and far between.

2 A *blanket*. The need for a blanket will become apparent within minutes of your first match. Cricket pitches are usually set in the middle of open spaces, occasionally with stunning views over open countryside. However, the wind speed and the distance viewed are directly linked and you will soon learn that a blanket to wrap around your legs is almost an essential.

3 An *umbrella or waterproof jacket*. The English spring/summer shower can frequently turn into a downpour, and whilst some schools will have a pavilion in which you can shelter, some pitches are set a long way from the main 1st XI pitch and you may need to seek refuge from the rain without the benefit of a building to protect you.

4 A *sleeping bag!* If you can stand your son's teasing, this is the ideal form of protection from wind and weather. It will keep you warm, protect you from the rain (so long as it has a waterproof outer cover) and will ensure that you can watch a complete match whatever the weather.

5 A *flask of hot tea or coffee*. Not all schools are able to provide tea for visiting supporters (especially when pitches are a long way from the school buildings or pavilion). Useful for staving off hypothermia!

6 *Snacks*. The match will often finish at nearly 7 o'clock and then there is a drive of anything up to two hours back home,

depending on the location of the opposition school and your own home's proximity to your son's school. If your son has homework to complete for school the next day, he will want to eat something on the journey, and although stopping for fish and chips might solve this problem, a bag of healthier snacks to keep his hunger at bay until you reach home can prove extremely useful.

7 *Sensible shoes.* Going to watch your son straight from work with your high heels and smart suit might seem a good idea on a lovely summer's day, but a pair of old 'flatties' in your car boot just for walking to the cricket field will prove invaluable.

A blanket is essential

Some Other Cricketing Terms

Commentators use the following on TV and radio.

Bowling a maiden over. Nothing to do with chatting up girls, this refers to an over in which the bowler succeeds in bowling all six balls without the batsman scoring any runs.

Caught and bowled. If a batsman hits the ball in such a way that the bowler can catch it before it touches the ground he is out *caught and bowled.*

Caught in the slips. If the batsman is caught by one of the players standing in the *slips* (see fielding diagram, p. 56) he is said to be *caught in the slips.*

Century. One hundred runs scored by one player.

Century stand. One hundred runs scored by two players together.

Double century. Two hundred runs by one player.

Getting his eye in. Refers to a batsman getting used to seeing the bowler bowling towards him and seeing the ball well (nothing to do with false eyes—although batsmen frequently replace contact lenses on the pitch these days and look as if they are replacing eyeballs!).

Getting off the mark. Refers to a batsman scoring his first run(s) in an innings.

Half century. Fifty runs by one player.

Hat tricks. If a bowler succeeds in taking three wickets with three successive balls, he is said to have taken a *hat trick*. After two balls he is *on a hat trick*.

Out leg before. The batsman is hit by the ball in such a way that if the ball had continued its path it would have connected with the wicket. He is therefore out *leg before wicket*. As previously explained he is not out if the ball hits his bat or glove first.

Out for a golden duck. The batsman gets out at the first ball he faces without scoring any runs.

Out for a duck. The batsman gets out without scoring any runs. The innovation of Kerry Packer and his Australian televised cricket matches has resulted in many TV companies using the picture of a sad duck waddling off the screen to accompany the batsman who is out for a duck on his return to the pavilion.

Stand. As in 'a fine stand', 'a century stand', etc. When two players stay together at the wicket during an innings and score a good number of runs between them, their stay at the wicket is called a stand. Usually innings only become stands after 50 runs have been scored.

A stand is also the area of seating for spectators and these can become muddled if you are listening to the radio. 'Sussex have a fine stand' could mean that two Sussex batsmen have played well together or that a new building has been completed and the spectators are now housed in new surroundings!

Scores. Listening to cricket commentaries on radio or watching a match on television, you will hear the score described in very specific ways. The batting side will have their score described using the number of runs they have scored first, followed by the number of wickets lost. So if a team has scored one hundred runs, but lost three wickets, the commentator would say, 'They are one hundred for three.' However, in Australia they often reverse this style and say 'three for one hundred'.

The fielding side would view this score as three for one hundred and the bowler's statistics are always described using the number of wickets taken first. If a bowler has taken all three of the wickets and only had twenty-five runs scored against him whilst bowling, his figures will be described by the commentators as three for twenty-five.

Because a match can be won either by scoring more runs or by losing fewer wickets, the results vary and a team can be described as having won the match by thirteen runs, or having beaten the opposition by three wickets. For instance:

X county scores 236 runs for 8 wickets
Y county scores 239 runs for 5 wickets
The result is that Y beat X by 5 wickets.

Another result could be:

X county scores 236 runs for 8 wickets
Y county scores 237 runs for 9 wickets
X county beats Y by 1 wicket.

Or alternatively:

X county scores 237 for 5
Y county scores 232 all out
X wins by 5 runs.

Scoring

Finally, if you are beginning to develop an interest in your son's game and want to have something more interesting to do during an afternoon's match—why not learn how to score?

The top of the score sheet shows the names of the opponents, the weather and pitch conditions, and the type of match and date it was played. In addition, there are separate sections for the batsmen, the bowlers and extra runs (no-balls, wides, etc.), and sections for special details such as run rates, for the batsmen, and details of the fall of wickets, including which member of the fielding side caused the wicket to fall, the time on the clock and the score at the time.

You will need to ask your fellow scorer, or the fielder standing closest, the bowler's names—if they are not your son's friends—and the boys waiting to bat will always supply the names of the batsmen.

In order to explain the scoring marks, let's start with the bowler's section at the bottom of the sheet (see p. 99). As you can see, the bowler gets each ball marked either with a small dot or with the number of runs scored off the ball. If he bowls a *no ball*, a circle is placed around the dot and an extra dot will appear in the box for that over. In addition a mark is made in the NO BALL section on the sheet.

If the bowler bowls a *wide*, a small x is marked in that over's box instead of a dot and a mark is placed in the WIDES section of the sheet.

Byes and *leg byes* are also marked in this section of the sheet and are marked against the bowler by the use of B for byes and LB for leg byes. When the number of runs scored against each bowler is added up the total should be equivalent to the number of runs scored by batsmen plus the extras (no balls, wides, byes and leg byes).

BYES	ı		1
LEG BYES	ıı		2
WIDES	ıııııııııı		10
NO BALLS	ııı ⊕ıⓄıı ııııı		11
		TOTAL	246
UMPIRES	B. MERCER		
	MR J. MOULTON		
SCORERS	D. SALES		
	K. GRAHAM		

Extras section from a score sheet. The total includes all the runs scored by batsmen as well

FALL OF WICKETS				
WKT NO.	SCORE AT FALL	BAT NO.	STAND OF	TIME OF WKT
1	89	2	89	5/33
2				
3				
4				
5				
6				
7				
8				
9				
10				
WICKETS		OVERS		
FOR	1	IN	39.3	
RESULT OF MATCH				
WIN				

Fall of wickets section from a score sheet

If the bowler takes a wicket this is marked with a small w in place of the dot on his line of details.

If the bowler has succeeded in bowling six balls without any runs being scored, this is called a *maiden* over, and the scorer marks this over with an M through the points for each of the six balls. If at the end of the over a wicket has been taken, the scorer marks through the six dots with a W shape on the bowler's entry, as long as no runs have been scored. This is called a *wicket maiden*.

Each batting innings has its own sheet and the score book is therefore made up of sets of two pages for each match played. The batsmen have a line each on which their runs are scored; balls which are faced but no runs scored are marked with a dot and anything from a single run to a six is marked appropriately.

Again, no balls are marked with a circle surrounding the dot and when runs are scored off a no ball the number is put inside the circle just as it is in the bowler's section. Some scorers will mark a maiden over against the batsman as well as showing it in the bowlers' section. This is done by joining the six dots in the batsman's score line together with an M shape as was done in the bowlers' record.

Leg byes and byes are also marked in the batsman's section to complete the picture and as he is out a small w is marked in his row, followed by two lines, marked in an arrow shape, to indicate that his innings is over (see p. 100).

The total score is marked off in two sections, the main section in the centre of the sheet marks off runs as they are scored and the rate per over section on the right hand side of the sheet gives an over by over latest score (see p. 101).

As if keeping up with this were not complicated enough, experienced (or should I say expert) scorers can give batsmen charts of where they have hit balls during their innings (see the sample on p. 102). These show where the batsman generally hits the ball and can help him to adjust his style to ensure that more runs are scored in future.

It is certainly true to say that if you learn to score for a

BOWLING ANALYSIS ALL NO BALLS AND WIDES NOW ATTRIBUTED AGAINST BOWLER

BOWLER	1	2	3	4	5	6	7	8	9	10	11	12	13	14	15	16	17	18	19	20	21	22	OVERS	MDNS	RUNS	WKTS
1 WALKER			M																				7	1	21	0
2 GARRETT																							7	0	49	0
3 WINN J.																							4.3	0	31	0
4 COLLENETTE																							4	0	18	1
5 FOOKS																							2	0	20	0
6 BECK																							3	0	20	0
7 STOKES																							2	0	18	0
8 BROCK OWEN																							5	0	40	0

The bowling analysis

	BATSMAN	TIME			RATE 50/100	HOW OUT	BOWLER	TOTAL
		IN	OUT					
1	WINTER J.	4/03	6/45	⟨scoring marks⟩	53θ 47M	NOT	OUT	78
2	HAYDOCK S.	4/03	5/33	⟨scoring marks⟩	61θ 7Im	CAUGHT @ROLK OWEN	COLLENETTE	36
3	SALES D.	5/34	6/45	⟨scoring marks⟩	75m 35θ 22.61 34θ 78m	NOT	OUT	108
4	SMITHERS J.			73θ 7Im				
5								
6								
7								
8								
9								
10								
11								

The batsmen's section of the score sheet

An example of the right hand side section of a score sheet

AT A GLANCE SCORE

The at a glance score

RATE PER OVER

OVER NO.	TOTAL SCORE	WICKETS	BOWLER NUMBER
1	1	0	1
2	2	0	2
3	4	0	1
4	8	0	2
5	8	0	1
6	13	0	2
7	14	0	1
8	16	0	2
9	22	0	1
10	34	0	2
11	39	0	1
12	49	0	2
13	51	0	3
14	56	0	4
15	64	0	3
16	67	0	4
17	71	0	3
18	73	0	4
19	81	0	3
20	89	1	4
21	97	1	5
22	101	1	6
23	113	1	5
24	122	1	6
25	128	1	1
26	136	1	6
27	139	1	7
28	154	1	2
29	169	1	7
30	178	1	8
31	188	1	7
32	190	1	8
33	194	1	7
34	204	1	8
35	206	1	7
36	208	1	8
37	218	1	7
38	231	1	8
39	238	1	7
40	246	1	3
41			
42			
43			
44			
45			
46			
47			
48			
49			
50			

Rate per over section

cricket team you will not only learn a lot more about the game, but will also concentrate a great deal more closely on what takes place and your enjoyment can often be increased as a result.

Name: SALES
Opponent: NORMANDY

Date 2/9/93
Conditions GOOD
Venue: GUILDFORD

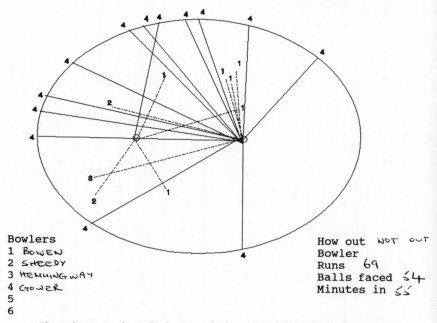

Bowlers
1 BOWEN
2 SHEEDY
3 HEMMINGWAY
4 GOWER
5
6

How out   NOT OUT
Bowler
Runs   69
Balls faced 54
Minutes in 55

Chart showing where the batsman hit his scoring shots during his innings

UMPIRE'S SIGNALS

In order for the scorer to be certain of what has happened after a ball is bowled, umpires have a set of special signals which they used to indicate specific events. I have already explained how the umpire shows that a batsman is out, by raising his index finger.

To indicate a wide ball he holds both arms out extended to the side and level with his shoulders.

To indicate a no ball he shouts loudly, 'No ball', and holds one arm only (normally his right arm) outstretched in the same way as he would for a wide.

A bye is shown by one arm being raised above his head. For a leg bye the umpire taps on his leg with his hand.

When four runs have been scored the umpire waves one arm from side to side at waist level (frequently oscillating his hand as if indicating a bumpy sea!).

For a six he will raise both arms straight above his head.

Four byes are indicated using a combination of the raised arm and the waving hand, while four leg byes obviously stretch the umpire's dexterity as he combines a four sign with his leg bye sign. One solution is to slap his thigh with one hand and wave the other hand.

Finally, the umpire indicates the end of each over by calling out 'over' so that the players (and hopefully the scorers) can hear.

Obviously the umpires need to know that the scorers have registered the unusual calls and signs and the scorers will therefore signal back to the umpire by waving a hand to show that they have been paying attention. Less experienced scorers sometimes forget this, since one hand will be holding the scorebook and the other will be busy writing down the details in three or four places on the page, and umpires often have to shout to make sure that their signs are acknowledged.

The umpires not only indicate the scores to the scorers but also act as coat hangers for the fielding team, wearing extra sweaters round their waists and clutching extra hats or sun glasses as and when required. They have a tough job to do in what can often be freezing conditions, and it is a wise umpire who learns the benefit of thermal underwear or extra layers of sweaters early in the season when the spring winds and weather can make standing for several hours umpiring a game of cricket an extremely unpleasant task.

Afterthought

'It's a funny kind of month, October. For the really keen cricket fan it's when you discover that your wife left you in May!'

Dennis Norden

I do hope you will be able to change this situation if your interest in cricket is truly kindled by this book, and that you may be able to go along with your husband or boyfriend and watch a match with renewed interest in future. At the very least I hope you will understand a little more about what your small son is trying to do out there in the middle of that field.